My Beloveds Promise

Trust what comes
Adventure is fun
Looking for the best
Provison for the test
The beauty that one
Can manifest.
Light comes not to rest
But shines so I can see
Drinking from this sea
Everlasting as I pass on
to a new illumined being.

By Ryan Daniels

Order this book online at www.trafford.com
or email orders@trafford.com

Most Trafford titles are also available at major online book retailers.

© Copyright 2007, 2011 Ryan Daniels.

All rights reserved. No part of this publication may be reproduced, stored in a retrieval system, or transmitted, in any form or by any means, electronic, mechanical, photocopying, recording, or otherwise, without the written prior permission of the author.

Note for Librarians: A cataloguing record for this book is available from Library and Archives Canada at www.collectionscanada.ca/amicus/index-e.html

Printed in the United States of America.

ISBN: 978-1-4251-1619-4

Trafford rev. 04/21/11

 www.trafford.com

North America & international
toll-free: 1 888 232 4444 (USA & Canada)
phone: 250 383 6864 ♦ fax: 812 355 4082

Precious Time

What you can't see
Is it hard to believe?
Because there it is
In the breeze
Whispering that you won't
Freeze in the cold
That the ground holds.
In your heart you are free
Look for the good deeds
It will come to be
The peace that we need.
Truth belongs
That we wait for so long
To find our mind
To help us align
With our precious time.

By Ryan Daniels

Honored

A world of creation
To manifest perfection
From the Divine
That guides us to be kind
To no end of time.
Love combines
Opportunity in our minds
Honored to know such beauty
From something that is so pure
It doesn't bring us tears
Just the real happiness
That our hearts revere
Because we are near.

By Ryan Daniels

Life

Face life
Don't let a moment
Pass you by
For there is no escape
Forever lasting it will go
It is better than having
A piece of gold.
Learn to let things change
There is more than fame
For what you may have
But life it self.
Take it far as it may be
Do what you love
Things will come to place
And you will see
What was meant for you
In the beginning of time
Of this earthly life of today.

By Ryan Daniels

The Divine Of A Rose

The sun shining bright
Showing from that height
The things that perish
Right in front of our sight.

Teaching detachment
And hold on to my inner light
To help with my next life.

This moment I need to grow
And taking this time to feed my soul
Asking to turn this seed into a rose
From the spring water that God holds.

By Ryan Daniels

Come Together

Far beyond our imagination

There is a great destination.

From our preparation

We will see the great dispensation

To help our situation

In this mass of complication

Of our own creation.

Open our heart

Let the universe

Contribute to our Nations!

By Ryan Daniels

Today

Watching the sun
Go down
With the waves
Crashing the ground
Understanding
The world turns around.
It really is meaningless
If we don't
Get the willingness
To ask to turn on
The switch
That doesn't miss
The truth
Which starts with
An unselfish deed.
The tools then appear
That help us to see
The meaning of the day
That we all live in
And peace will not fade!

By Ryan Daniels

Two Alike

Heart and mind
Must combine
To find the divine
See with your eyes
You don't have to die.
The joy it brings
You want to sing
And soar with
Your new wings
In all things!

By Ryan Daniels

Focus

When you fail

Don't be discouraged then bail

One day you will prevail.

Stay on the glorious path

That is life's trail

Pray for the lift

Of your veils.

Watch for your clear vision

Think wisely of your decisions

And rejoice in your mission.

By Ryan Daniels

Independent Sight

God is what creates
Which is our fate
We can't anticipate
Must increase our love
To those who hate
Because God asks
Us to love for His sake.
As we pass the gate
Open to us straight
From the essence
Of our good traits
From the wine of love
That has infinite taste
Helping us to witness
The Divine that is
So gloriously great.

By Ryan Daniels

Humble

In the time of need
I plead to be free
Allow my good deeds
To be the tree
That I can be.
Share an open me
To people that love Thee
In my community.
So my fruit can give opportunity
As I speak sincerly
With my perfect being
Longs even more for the bounties
When I recite Thee
Because it is shown openly
What is meant for me!

By Ryan Daniels

Follow Yourself

Open your heart
Show your art
Watch it become a part
Of its decoration
Of creation.
Watch it flow
Like the wind blows
Through the meadow
Be at peace with it
Watch it grow
Follow forward
To your inspiration,
There is a destination.

By Ryan Daniels

World Wind

As you cry out
Forget the doubt
Because there
Is always help.
Open to us
When we burst
Through the winds
That tries to
Keep us pinned.
God comes within
And helps us win!

By Ryan Daniels

Love Is Might

Praying through the night
And look for the
Breaking daylight
Without it
We wouldn't have life.
Love with all
Your might
This is what makes
Us right
With a world
That grows bright
Every time
The love gets tight.

By Ryan Daniels

Find Your Heart

Find your way
To true sight
It will bring you
To such height.
Explore the freedom
Within the kingdom
Peace will come
Within them.
When love
Hits the heart
It finds you internal
Then you begin
To know who you are.
Far as it may be
It is closer
Once it's shown to thee.

By Ryan Daniels

Home

As you walk tall
Don't fall
Into the hands
Of those that are
Taking what they can.
Be closer to the kingdom
Where there is freedom
In the hearts of men
That do comprehend
Because there is no end
Just God's friends
Come and join in.

By Ryan Daniels

Who We Are

An open heart
With radiance
Shows God is not far
Working on the light
Of who we are.
We got plenty
Of what we need
For God is Free
The World is limited
Because it is meant to be.
Heading on adventures
With each prayer
I am able to create
Which is not fake
With every letter I see
I know it's no mistake.

By Ryan Daniels

Contentment

The light of day
Will be the same
When the highest
Sight is attained.

Soar through the night
With no fright
When the lights shine bright
You know life is tight.

Look nowhere to be found
For you're bound to life
Once around.
So make it right
Because there is nothing
But internal light.

Be true to who you are
Without blame
And hope
Will spread like a flame.

By Ryan Daniels

Open Your Heart

Speak from the heart
It will take you far
Because people wish
To know who you are.
The good they hear
Because you are near
Hoping that you
Will come and
Show no fear
Because God
Created the atmosphere!

By Ryan Daniels

Trust

The hearts of men
Are in a playpen
Free thyself from dust
And trust there is more
That your eyes
Wish to explore.
It's the heart that
Will open the door
Who will continue
With that dance?
Happy be that man
With that chance
Through his might
Looking inside
Seeing that light
That we pass
With each other
No matter what class!

By Ryan Daniels

It Will Come

What you can't find
Will grow to be found
Take it when you can
See it to be true
In your hands
And see what life
Has in hold for you.
Laugh and fly
On a natural high
Dance when you can
Groove to what
Your spirit tells you.
Hold your head high
Look people in the eye
Keep your heart open
To what may come.

By Ryan Daniels

Movement

I glide without notice
Because I'm focused
And never knew
The distance I've come
In the scales of my thoughts
I ought to be smiles!
The whispers
I hear in the breeze
Make me freeze
But it's the glowing heart
That one feels
To help the choice become real.

By Ryan Daniels

Asking Boldly

Asking why
Is like saying
Good-bye?
Not in my eyes
I see the beauty
When the holy
Moves boldly
Through the fragrance
Not in vengeance.
To build a Heavenly residence
Which begins when
I pay attention
Like what we inherit
From our beautiful parents.

By Ryan Daniels

Breath Of Life

Holding something beautiful
Is not false
When there is a pulse
Through humanity
Truth is not an illusion
When the eyes
Of the hearts
Are included within,
The world that we live in.
Enjoying the breath
Which shows no effort
Like a family
In the spirit of life
That will last forever.

By Ryan Daniels

Wisdom Of One's Tree

The fruits of a tree
Help us to understand free
Within our own minds
Not to confine the growth
That happens in time.
Open to us to find
That sprit and food combine
Helps with body and soul
So that you can grow old.
Share your wisdom
From the Majestic Kingdom
Who is bold to ask where
Did you get this gold?

By Ryan Daniels

In My World

Give and receive
With joy that believes
It is the Divine
That helps combine
Two sides in unity
See it to be true
It is in you.

By Ryan Daniels

Bright Lights

Life is beautiful
See it to be true
Don't be a fool
Soul grows with you.
Let the light shine
Be kind
Because you know who
Will be flowing through
Your mind.
An understanding of why
When that time passes by
The voice of reason
Will come no matter
What season.
Start with a light
It will ignite
Seen from the heavens
Radiant so bright.

By Ryan Daniels

Peace Of Mind

Stay on the lighted path

Everything is like a flash

Seeing through

Like an hourglass.

Then you start to laugh

Because you learn

God's wisdom

Then the bounties come with them

Because the kingdom is open!

By Ryan Daniels

Oh My Lord

As I manifest
My Lord's work
It will show
Its colors of glory
Then I will start
Not to worry.
I'm not alarmed
Of the flurry
Because I'm armed
With love
Contributed from above.
That is found in the heart
Growing to the stars
As the clouds disappear
In the midnight atmosphere
Knowing that the
Sun is still shining
Because the heaven
Is twinkling bright
And the moon
Is giving us light.

By Ryan Daniels

What's Knocking?

Glory comes knocking
On your door
Which takes you
Nowhere but forward
Turn the doorknob
Out of the wonderment
For the truth.
That comes to question
Is it really yours?
Appearing only in a form that
You never thought it would be
It's only your mind that struggles
With opening the door.
But your heart already feels
What's on the other side
Is it really life?
Is it the illusion that your mind thinks?
One day it will come to your door
And the glory will be all yours
That is if you can be
The person that you want to see.

By Ryan Daniels

Explore With An Open Mind

Open our mind
Don't let it be confined
To something that perishes.
A power tool
Don't be a fool
It helps us like food
When you feed the mind
The good that it wishes
Otherwise you will
Be doing the dishes.
But with an open mind
You will find the signs
That your heart designs.

By Ryan Daniels

Change In Sight

A winding road
That it may be
Imprisoned in the life
That we weave
Short as lives will be
But we still desire to be free.
The hearts of men
Will become friends
In a new life
That has no end.

By Ryan Daniels

Free As Dreams

When you're single
It's a great time to mingle
But first you must learn
How not to get burned
From a world that is on fire
Listen to your hearts' desire.
Wait for the truth
It will come to root,
Patience is the key
Because it is a good deed.
Your hopes and dreams
Will become free
Because your reality
Is meant to be.

By Ryan Daniels

Be A Friend

When you want
A friend
You must
See the end
And be a friend.
Don't worry
About being a ten
Be yourself
It takes the doubt
And flushes it out.
Enjoy the bond
Because how long
It will last
Only God can grasp.

By Ryan Daniels

Freedom

When a group
Can be true friends
It's like it has no end
You can share
Who you are
Without being dared.
Free of fear
That becomes clear
When you show up here
Without a beer
We can grow and cheer
Even if there is a tear!

By Ryan Daniels

Burning Fire

As I fall to my knees
I plead to peel
From the fire that burns
And there is no where to turn
But to the heavens above
Asking for the cup
That is full of mercy.
As I cry
My soul dives
In the ocean
Of forgiveness
Short as it may be
Life is full of dreams.
The reality of your burdens
Are free when you think
Positively!

By Ryan Daniels

Glory

The Friend with kindness
Is attaining
Everlasting happiness.
Hope and dreams
Is what I create
And it is not fake.
What I want
Is my heart's design
And that is not from me
It is not far away.
The light that
Is strong inside
Just open my eyes
God will show
And that is no lie.

By Ryan Daniels

Where Am I

When I look
Around
And all I see
Is the ground
I can't be found
Because I am
Feeling down.

Be happy
That I'm human
For I am blooming
In a garden
That is never farther
Than the river water.
Many flowers true
But it is meant to be
God can see, yes
That it is me!

By Ryan Daniels

Unexpected Battle

I found myself in a bout
With a lot of doubt
Unaware of the help
Days grew scarier
All I had was
An invisible barrier.
Heart and mind
Were in a bind
It was hard to find
Without my mind.
By the way I did pray
And help did find its way
Now again I can see
The light of day!

By Ryan Daniels

Open Air

Free to fly where I don't die
Nor have to hide
Truth grows and it shows
In our own lives
As I open my eyes.
My being fills with light
When I don't lie
Don't say good-bye
God, I see your signs by my side.
Guiding my existence
With infinite insight
With every step of happiness
As He is Patiently waiting
Watching us in open daylight
Sending every letter that
Fills my heart with such love,
That releases the fresh air
That we can all bear
From something that is Inherent!

By Ryan Daniels

What Was Meant To Be

To know where
I have been destined to be
Serving the Prince of Peace
Asking for what
My Master wishes for me
Staying radiant with God's Will.

Strength comes from the King
Sending innate knowledge
To create in the home
Which stirs up in the bones
As the opportunity grows
Asking to have love in the heart
So more can be revealed!

By Ryan Daniels

Strength Within

As fear is on all sides
You trust what is inside
You find the strength
It is like a tank.
Look for the good
That will lead the way
Like sunlight in the day.
Smell the flowers
It is clean
Like the summer showers
Joy is found
In something so profound!

By Ryan Daniels

True Might

What is on my heart?
Directs me as I pray
Not for hate
That is what dissipates
With every word
As I recite the understanding
Of the infinite might.
From the Divine assistance
That is the witness
Of our existence
Holding me in heights
Making sure the impurity
Is not the hype.
I am loving and wishing
For the well being
Of every human in sight.
There is no time to waste
Truth will not wait
It is visible like a spring day
When we say it the right way.
It is already made
Not from ourselves
But what God
Has put on my bookshelf!

By Ryan Daniels

My Spot

I have found a spot
That cannot
Be forgot
It has what's
In my heart with
The Beauty of nature
Of God's art.
Shown to me
Not by the stars
But through my search
That is not far.
Reading the growth
That helps me to bare fruit
That comes from the roots
Where I was told
How to feed my soul!

By Ryan Daniels

Coming To Light

When you have the insight
To know how
To help someone's life
The smiles it brings
The joy it sings
It cannot be forgotten
Because it's always talking
How wonderful it was
That you were there.
To show your true light
In great heights
In that person's life.

By Ryan Daniels

Witnessed

What did appear
On a snowy day of the year?
Two dear angels
To help clear
An old lady's walk way.
The little girls
Happy that they are
To earn money
For a chocolate bar
And it didn't matter how
Little they are.
The joy that my friend saw
came to be
Amazing to see
It warmed my heart
When he shared it with me!

By Ryan Daniels

Angel Ways

When the angel
Is dancing life is good
Profound when the angel
Sings their sounds.
Blue or gray
Angels will see the way
On a high mountain
Nothing blocks your way
When you see life's obstacles
Always remember
An angel comes to your aid.
Fly and soar
For life is so yours.

By Ryan Daniels

Living Health

Work the body art

Which helps the heart.

Strong is what you want

Here's the magic wand

Set your goals

That's where to go

It is no fools' gold.

Don't give up the journey

Because it is early

To earn success

You must take that step

So don't forget true material wealth

Is to have good health!

By Ryan Daniels

Potency

I love my body
It is blooming
As I work it
It is not perfect.
As I keep it healthy
It is allowing me
To develop
What is meant to be
That is to
Manifest good deeds.
The Divine Teachings
Are free
It is wonderful to see
Because I believe openly
Beaming as I drink
From the sea
And wait patiently.
It will always come
But you can't see
Until you dive
Into His Teachings.

By Ryan Daniels

Good Night

When we glide under
The moonlight
And we see the stars
Twinkling bright
We know there is life
Beyond the night.
But it is so nice
When we see the ocean
Ripple through the depths
An amazing sight
That burns through the daylight.
When it reaches midnight
We will sleep right
Knowing the sun is coming up
It gives us sight
When we wake before the night.

By Ryan Daniels

Golden

As life moves along
It comes in many songs
When your heart lifts
You know she has a gift.
As I may not see
But I know it has to be
For she is golden to me.
One day we will meet
Then ask me
Why so long
Until you sang this song.
I will reply
In God's eyes
I have been waiting for
Her to be by my side.

By Ryan Daniels

Two Of Me

As I walk
No matter what talk
I discover what makes
My heart brighter
Because it is higher
Than one thought.
As I fought
The inner being
And seeing
What it is made of
Not for fame
Just my sweet dame!
Dreams are one way
That make it tame
But what was said
Thats what came
The throne of the heart
Is God's Art.

By Ryan Daniels

Soul Food

Feed the mind
Grows the soul
Doesn't matter
How old.
This is what
We need to know
This is what
We hold.
If you grasp
It will last
It is a task
When you ask
So don't dash
Because it's
Better than cash.

By Ryan Daniels

Service In Life

To grasp what it might be
Yes it is a dream
It can be wonderful
When achieved.
Look towards something
That gives you delight
With the service
That gives you flight
Because that is what
The world needs
No matter what walk of life.

By Ryan Daniels

The Start

When you reach the base
Of a mountain
It gives you height
And goals that you might
Not have had in sight.
When you show
You never know
Where it will go.
But if you didn't show
You won't have those goals
Shoot that fear
For it won't disappear
Until you appear
With the assistance
That you ask from a distance!

By Ryan Daniels

Igniting The Way

A striving force
Of a community
When there is unity
Which starts
With the inner being
And shared
With the human beings.

unity

Light the fire
That ignites
The entire truth
Don't be blind
With faith search
Every which way
Because your heart
Is with today!

By Ryan Daniels

Choice Of Heart

Choice by Heart
It is like a dart
That blossoms together
The peoples vision
Not like television.
Breaks through
The mind that
Can make us blind
To the beauty that shines.
When love combines
You will find the Divine!

By Ryan Daniels

Your Search

Search your heart
You will know there
Is more to life
Than just your own part
Of your creation.
A universe to explore
Unlimited with no bore
Be happy and smile
There is more
Open your mind
There is much to find.
Be kind because
There is lots of time!

By Ryan Daniels

Counsels Of Perfection

The language arts

"I hope thou wilt acquire great proficiency in writing literature, composition, eloquence of tongue and fluency of speech"..

Tablets Vol. 3, p. 501

"Endeavour, so far as it is possible for thee, that day by day thou mayest string the pearls of poesy with sweeter rhythm and more eloquent contents"...

Tablets Vol. 3, p. 546

"The Bab subsequently quoted this well-known tradition: 'Treasures lie hidden beneath the throne of God: the key to those treasures is the tongue of poets.' "

Dawn-Breakers, pp. 258 – 9 (U.K. edn., p. 181)

Counsels Of Perfection
Author Genevieve Coy
p. 114

Writings From Baha'i Faith

www.ingramcontent.com/pod-product-compliance
Lightning Source LLC
Chambersburg PA
CBHW041529220426
43671CB00002B/36